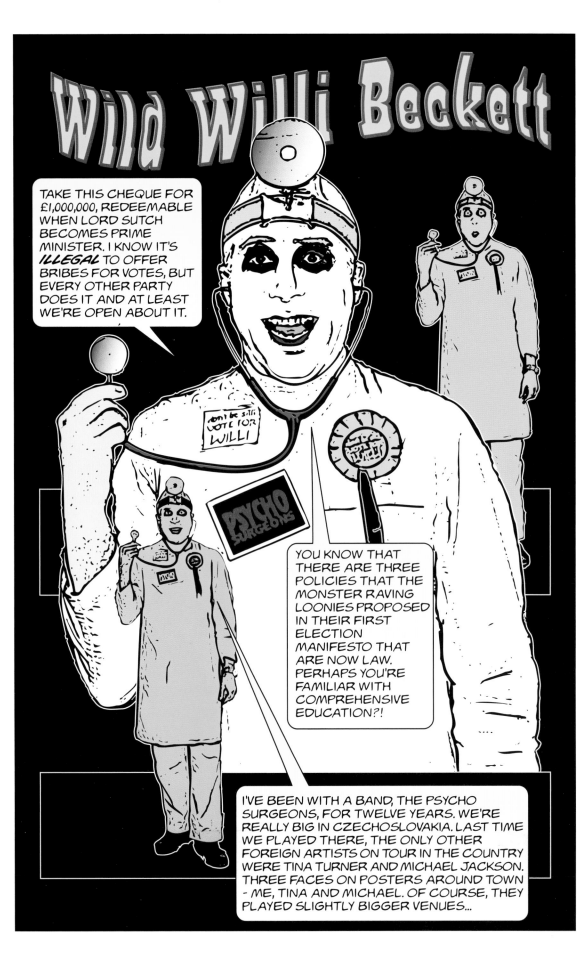

Alan Biggin

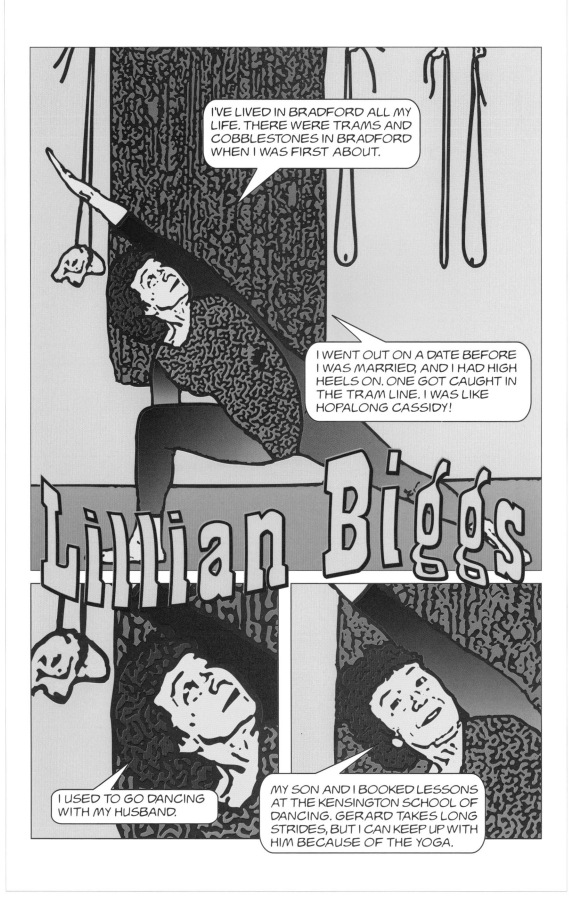

Dustbin Dave

I'VE BEEN ON THE BINS FOR 22 YEARS, SO I KNOW THE JOB A BIT NOW. IT'S A FEW MILES IS THAT. I WOULDN'T LIKE TO WORK IT OUT.

AFTER WORK I LIKE TO GO FOR A PINT, DO A BIT OF *GARDENING*. I USED TO GARDEN FOR OTHER PEOPLE A BIT.

PEOPLE KNOW MY FACE. THEY SAY THEY'VE MET ME BEFORE, THEN I TELL THEM THAT I'M ON THE BINS.

Dennis Flatt

YOU KNOW I WAS A PHOTOGRAPHER. I WAS BROUGHT UP WITH HEAVY PLATE CAMERAS. ANYONE WITH A 35MM WAS A REAL AMATEUR THEN.

I STARTED ABOUT 1950. I WORKED AS A PRINTER CORRECTING EVERYONE'S MISTAKES. I STILL PHOTOGRAPH A LITTLE BIT FOR MYSELF. LETS JUST SAY I HELP OUT THE DIOCESIAN NEWSPAPER. BACK THEN I USED TO BE A REAL RUGBY FANATIC. IN 1986 I BECAME THE BRITISH NIKON PRESS PHOTOGRAPHER OF THE YEAR. I WAS THE ONLY PROVINCIAL PHOTOGRAPHER TO HAVE BEEN IT AT THE TIME.

OH, I'M ALSO A KEEN GARDENER - THAT'S FOR MR HOLDSWORTH, HE'LL KNOW WHAT I MEAN.

DR Les Goldman

I'VE BEEN A G.P. IN BRADFORD FOR 13 YEARS NOW. I'VE GOT THREE KIDS AND LIKE TO SPEND A LOT OF TIME WITH THEM. WE HAVE TWO CATS, SOME GERBILS AND 5 CHICKENS. OUTSIDE WORK, IT'S MUSIC THAT KEEPS ME GOING.

I'VE PLAYED THE SAXOPHONE FOR ABOUT 10 YEARS. I ALSO PLAY CLARINET. I'M IN A NUMBER OF BANDS - ALL AMATEUR OF COURSE. I LOVE IT. IT'S A REAL CHALLENGE.

I THINK THAT I'M HERE BECAUSE OF MY WORK AS A G.P. WITH HOMELESS PEOPLE IN BRADFORD. I SEE THE PROBLEMS OF HOMELESSNESS GETTING STEADILY WORSE. THERE ARE MORE AND MORE HOMELESS YOUNG PEOPLE. ALSO THERE'S AN EXPLODING DRUG PROBLEM.

MANY G.P.'S ARE WORKING VERY HARD IN THE FACE OF DISTRESS AND DIFFICULTY. MY HOMELESS PEOPLE'S SURGERY IS ABOUT TO BE REBUILT, THOUGH, AND THAT MAKES ME FEEL REALLY OPTIMISTIC.

Jim Greenhalf

I'VE WORKED FOR THE TELEGRAPH & ARGUS FOR 20 YEARS AS A FEATURE WRITER AND COLUMNIST.

I WRITE ABOUT A VARIETY OF THINGS: FOOTBALL, POLITICS. I'VE MADE MYSELF VERSATILE. MY JOB IS TO KNOW ABOUT A LOT OF THINGS OR TO FIND OUT ABOUT THEM IN SHORT ORDER.

JOURNALISM IS A MYSTERIOUS PROFESSION. THERE'S NO OBJECTIVE TRUTH - A GOOD JOURNALIST IS NOT AFRAID TO COME DOWN ON A SIDE. FACTS HAVE TO BE INTERPRETED, OTHERWISE, YOU'RE JUST A NOTE TAKER.

A GOOD JOURNALIST PUTS INTO WORDS THE PUBLIC MOOD - RENDERING COMPLEX SITUATIONS AVAILABLE TO THE GENERAL PUBLIC.

THE JOURNALIST'S MOST IMPORTANT ROLE IS TO ACT AS A *LIGHTNING ROD*

Dr Gupta

I CAME TO THE U.K. 30 YEARS AGO. BRADFORD IS A SECOND HOME NOW. THERE WAS NO ASIAN LADY DOCTOR AND A LARGE ASIAN POPULATION. I'VE BEEN ORGANISING DAY TRIPS FOR PENSIONERS FOR 6 YEARS NOW. THE SMILE ON THEIR FACES WHEN THEY RETURN IS WORTH ALL THE EFFORT.

YOU CAN JUST GET OUT INTO THE COUNTRYSIDE. I USED TO DO THAT A LOT, BEFORE IT GOT TOO BUSY.

I READ A BIT - DAPHNE DU MAURIER IS ONE OF MY FAVOURITES. I LIKE READING ASTROLOGY. I'VE BEEN INTERESTED IN ASTROLOGY SINCE A CHILD.

WHEN YOU'RE EXAMINING A PATIENT, IT'S 'OCCULT'. THERE'S MAGIC IN IT. IF SOMEONE HAS PAIN, AND IT IS GONE, YOU JUST TELL BY THEIR FACE.

Janet Hobson

I'VE JUST REACHED MY HALF-CENTURY. 40 WAS WORSE. I FELT A BIT DOWN AT 40.

I'VE WORKED AT THE CATHEDRAL CENTRE FOR 18 MONTHS.

I WORKED FOR A BUILDING SOCIETY, AND I BECAME A VICTIM OF STRESS. SO I WENT TO DO A PAINTING COURSE AT THE CENTRE.

ON THE TOUR ROUND, I SAW THEY WERE ASKING FOR VOLUNTEERS TO TEACH ENGLISH LANGUAGE SKILLS.

SO I STARTED TEACHING. I'VE ALWAYS BEEN ABLE TO COMMUNICATE... WELL NOT ALWAYS - I WAS SHY AS A CHILD.

Patrick Howley

Edward Kalinowski
I WAS BORN IN POLAND AND I CAME HERE DURING THE WAR. I SERVED WITH THE POLISH ARMY IN SCOTLAND. AFTER DEMOB, I MOVED TO BRADFORD IN 1949.
I WAS AN OVERLOOKER IN TEXTILE. IN THOSE DAYS THE WHOLE CITY WAS WOOLEN. BUT THOSE DAYS ARE GONE. AFTER THAT I WORKED IN LOCAL GOVERNMENT, FOR RECREATION DIVISION.
I'M INVOLVED IN LOCAL FOOTBALL. THIS IS MY 38TH YEAR AS A REFEREE - I'M OVER 70. I ALSO PLAYED AS A PROFESSIONAL.
TWEEE!
THE PLAYERS ARE OK, BUT IF I GET ANY HASSLE I TELL 'EM "IF I WANT ANY HASSLE, I'LL GO SHOPPING." THEY USUALLY SEE THE FUNNY SIDE OF IT.
I'VE PROBABLY REFEREED DADS, SONS AND GRANDADS.

I CAME HERE TO HELP WITH THE RAVES. THERE WERE ONLY ABOUT A DOZEN OF THEM, BUT THEY WERE REALLY GREAT.

I KNEW PEOPLE HERE ANYWAY. I STARTED A MAGAZINE CALLED THE **BOOK OF LIES**, DID THREE ISSUES. I HAVEN'T DONE MUCH FOR A FEW YEARS NOW. I REALLY LOVE DOING ABSOLUTELY NOTHING. IT GIVES YOU TIME TO GO TO LOTS OF PARTIES.

I WAS DRIVING DOWN THE STREET THIS MORNING AND I SAW A BIRD FLY UP AND DO A PERFECT BARREL-ROLL, JUST FOR THE HELL OF IT. IT POINTED SOMETHING OUT TO ME, SO I'M DRIVING TO SEE MY BROTHER IN ABOUT HALF AN HOUR...

Jonathan Lamb

I'VE LIVED IN OTLEY MOST OF MY LIFE. SINCE 1986 THAT IS. I LIKE OTLEY. THERE'S LOTS OF SPACE TO PLAY OUT. I'VE GOT A MOUNTAIN BIKE.

LOADS OF FRIENDS LIVE IN BRADFORD. I LIKE IT. WE GO SHOPPING IN THE CENTRE OF TOWN.

I THINK I'D LIKE TO BE AN *AIRLINE PILOT*. I LIKE THE IDEA OF FLYING. I ALSO LIKE COOKING, THE IDEA OF TOSSING THINGS IN THE PAN.

I'M WELL KNOWN BECAUSE I SAVED MY DAD'S LIFE WHEN HE ACCIDENTALLY SEVERED AN ARTERY. I DON'T REALLY LIKE EVERYONE TO KNOW ABOUT ME AT SUCH A YOUNG AGE. IT'S NOT SUCH A BIG DEAL.

GURPAUL SANDHU

I'VE BEEN IN BRADFORD FOR 32 YEARS - I CAME HERE FROM THE *PUNJAB*.

WHEN I ARRIVED THERE WAS REAL CULTURE SHOCK. THERE WERE CHIMNEYS EVERYWHERE, SO I STARTED TO PHOTOGRAPH THEM AS A WAY OF COMING TO TERMS WITH THE NEW ENVIRONMENT. I'M VERY INTERESTED IN PHOTOGRAPHY.

THINGS ARE REALLY DIFFERENT HERE NOW. MOST PEOPLE UNDERSTAND HOW IMPORTANT IT IS FOR EVERYONE TO WORK TOGETHER.

I HAVE THREE HEROES: JOGEET SINGH CHITRA, THE CLASSICAL MUSICIAN, BOY GEORGE AND NELSON MANDELA. WHEN BOY GEORGE FIRST APPEARED, MY FAMILY WERE AMAZED THAT I LIKED HIM, THEY THOUGHT THAT HIS TYPE OF THING WASN'T FOR ME. BUT I THINK THAT HE'S MARVELLOUS.

Robina Siddique

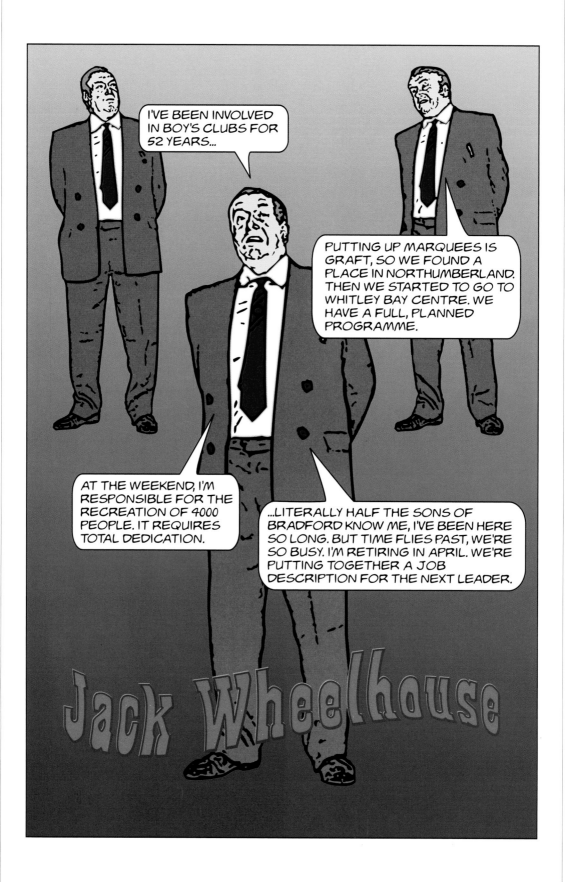

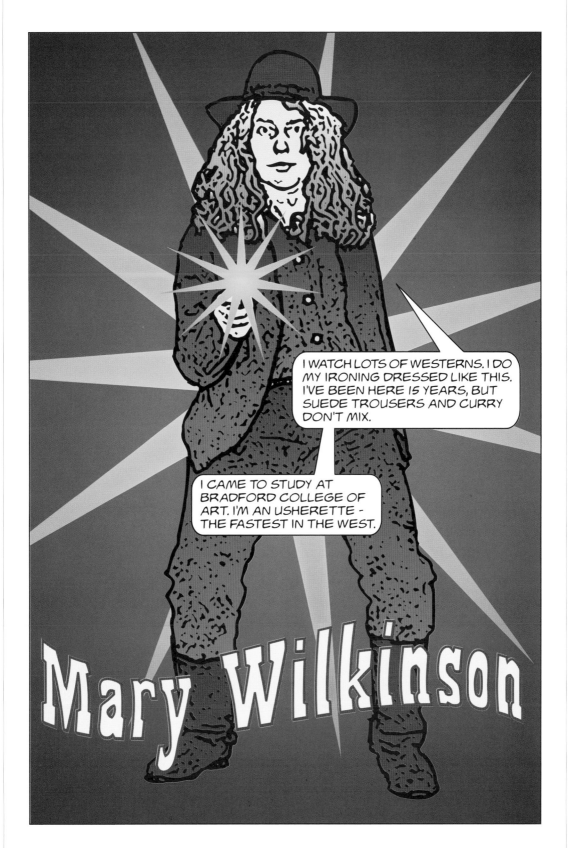

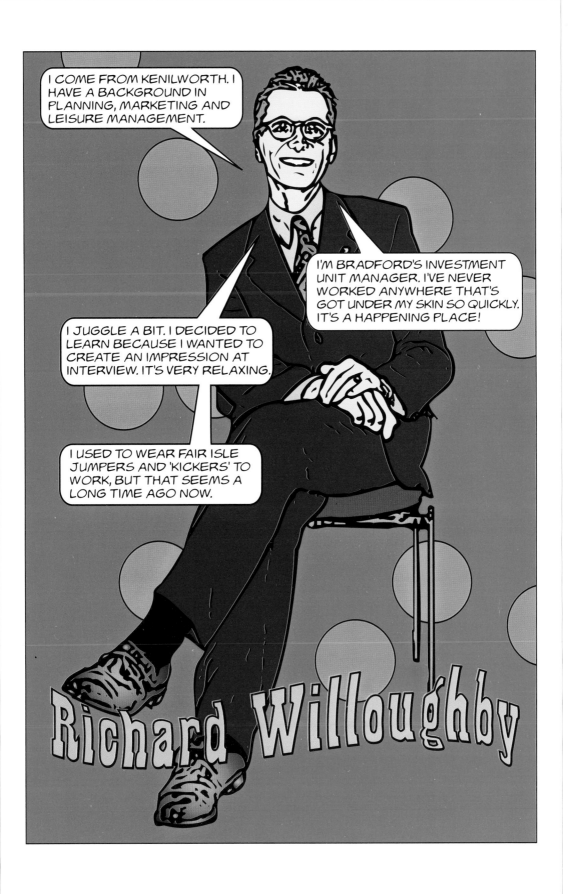

Acknowledgements

THANKS TO ALL THE 100 FOR THEIR PATIENCE AND KIND CO-OPERATION. WE HAD A BLAST...

RIGHT ON. WE'RE SURE THAT YOU DID TOO. THANKS FOLKS.

WE'D LIKE TO THANK THE NATIONAL MUSEUM OF PHOTOGRAPHY, FILM & TELEVISION AND BRADFORD & NORTHERN HOUSING ASSOCIATION WHO WORKED IN PARTNERSHIP WITH THE MUSEUM TO MAKE THIS PROJECT POSSIBLE. VERY SPECIAL THANKS GREG AND AMANDA. BRADFORD & NORTHERN HOUSING ASSOCIATION IS DELIGHTED TO JOIN BRADFORD'S SALUTE TO 100 VERY SPECIAL PEOPLE.

WE'D ALSO LIKE TO THANK THE FOLLOWING PEOPLE FOR KEEPING THE FAITH FOR SO LONG:- PAT GRENNAN, ELAINE WALKER, ROBERT BROWN, D.J. SIMPSON, CAITLIN MASLEY, VAL WILLIAMS, MICHAEL COLLINS, ALISON CROSBY, PAUL BROWNRIDGE, MICHAEL MACK, BEV BYTHEWAY, PAUL DILLON, PETER GOZINYA, ALAN WARD, ANDREW CROSS, TONY CLANCY, STELLA GIBBONS, DANIEL MEADOWS, EDWARD DENT, BARBARA & HOWARD MORSE, GARY GROTH, OPAL SPERANDIO, COLIN DE LAND, JOSHUA DECTER, GEORGE BARBERO, AC2 K, & NANCY PRINCENTHAL. AND THE MANY THAT WE MUST HAVE FORGOTTEN TO MENTION. EMAIL US AT SPERANDIO@AOL.COM! GRENNAN & SPERANDIO ARE REPRESENTED BY AMERICAN FINE ARTS, 22 WOOSTER STREET, NY, NY 10013 ☎ 212-941-0401